S0-BXX-420

Movies Made In Ireland

MICHAEL COLLINS

By Aubrey Dillon-Malone

GLI Limited
The Tower Enterprise Centre
Pearse Street
Dublin 2, Ireland
Tel: +353 1 6775655
Fax: +353 1 6775487
E-Mail: towerctr@iol.ie

First published by GLI Limited, 1996
© GLI Limited

© Text Copyright A. Dillon-Malone
Editor: Pat Neville
Typesetting & Layout: Alan Smyth Studios

ISBN: 1 900480 25 5

ACKNOWLEDGMENTS
The Star
Arthur Flynn
The Ballymena Guardian
The Examiner

Cover © A.Flynn

CONTENTS

Aidan Quinn, Julia Roberts, Liam Neeson and Alan Rickman (Copyright: The Examiner)

MICHAEL COLLINS

Starring:
Liam Neeson
Julia Roberts
Alan Rickman
Aidan Quinn
Stephen Rea
Ian Hart
Charles Dance
Jonathan Rhys Myers
Gerard McSorley

Director:
Neil Jordan

Year: 1996

INTRODUCTION

Michael Collins was one of Ireland's latterday super heroes, a man who cheated death so often he might have been protected by some spiritual force before the fatal ambush at mBéal na Bláth in 1922. He had always intuited it would be his own who would mow him down after all the years evading British Intelligence.

It was an irony that crowned an ironic life, but Irish history would never be the same after him. We had lost a man who seemed as comfortable at the negotiating table as he was ducking and diving round the streets of Dublin, or attending funerals of dead republican friends in only light disguise. A man who had lived most of his short life with a death sentence of one form or another hanging over his head, who epitomised the ideals of defiance and dependability, a pin-up for guerillas the world over.

If he had lived, he probably would have become another genial statesman like de Valera. He would also probably have lost the fire in his belly. The fact that he died in his prime means he can be captured forever in that dramatic freeze-frame: a man who refused to bend the knee even when all occasions did conspire against him. After all the hiccups and false starts in the thick rain of our troubled history, we deserved a hero like this.

The idea of making a film about him was fraught with difficulty. What kind of Michael Collins was director Neil Jordan going to serve up to the public?

Everybody had an angle on Collins. Every pubstool prophet and drawing-room dilettante. He was like a piece of litmus paper filtered through the prism of the collective Irish psyche. Either demi-god or anti-christ, depending on which side of the fence you fell on. Or your father did.

The bottom line was: no portrayal could satisfy everyone. You would make enemies whichever way you threw the dice. The secret was to let the visual image supersede all that: to make the audience forget you were giving them an unofficial history lesson.

Jordan tilted the balance in favour of Collins and against De Valera, the man who arguably shafted him. This was dangerous territory for those (and there were many) who believed Dev could walk on water without too much difficulty. But then so could Collins...depending on where you stood.

One man died in his prime; the other went on to become a living legend. Both were equally manipulative in their ways, but

Alan Rickman, who plays Eamon De Valera.
(*Copyright: The Star*)

only one of them was a folk hero. And now he was about to be immortalised in a different way. On celluloid.

Jordan said the movie was closer to him than any he made before, despite (or maybe because of) the heartache it caused him. 'I have never lost more sleep over the making of a film than I have over *Michael Collins*', he said, adding, 'But I'll never make a more important one either.' It was, he said, 'the untold story of the country', the internecine squabbling of high-ranking politicians thrown into high relief by the gunmen who shed blood for a hazy ideal.

From a more pragmatic point of view, people wondered if former *wunderkind* prose-poet Jordan had enough experience under his directorial belt (not to mention steady historical perspective) to handle the controversial material in a manner that would grip the public while still remaining broadly faithful to events as they

Garrett Flynn poses for the camera in
Carlisle Grounds, Bray.   (*Copyright*: A. *Flynn*)

happened, bearing in mind that such events would be in living memory to some, and handed down verities to a latter generation of Jordan's own vintage.

Could Jordan, a dreamer of dreams and weaver of abstruse and sometimes solipsistic images, keep his tendency towards self-indulgence at bay for a three-hour rollercoaster ride through a socio-political minefield?

As a critic in *Empire* magazine pointed out, in a preview of the film, 'The high-calibre talent is certain to get it noticed, but 70-year old Anglo-Irish politics is likely to slam this in the box marked 'Difficult'.

This was probably the biggest understatement since Noah said it looked like rain.

A city in disarray - technicians at work.
(Copyright: *The Examiner*)

BIRTHPANGS

If Michael Collins thought negotiating with David Lloyd George was difficult, he should have tried making a movie about himself. Jordan spent over a decade trying to get it off the ground, fighting his own mini War of Independence with the moguls.

The screenplay languished in dry dock for many years, as low a priority for those who hold the purse-strings of the movie industry as it was a labour of love for its writer/director.

The miracle was that Jordan got it up and running at all. Like his hero Collins, he found himself fighting an uphill battle with the larger forces of a dubious bureaucracy. He had been advised to cry off the project many times before, the 'suits' feeling a biopic about a relatively obscure Irish

The real Michael Collins (*Copyright: The Star*)

military hero wouldn't entrance the public in the same way as say , an Arnold Schwarzenneger blockbuster.

History, as Henry Ford once opined, was bunk.

Jordan was no stranger to political material, of course, his 1982 directorial debut being the highly charged A*ngel*, about a troubled saxaphonist (Stephen Rea) who takes to the gun after being traumatised by voilence himself. Producer David Puttman actually commissioned Jordan to do a Collins script after seeing A*ngel*. But such a script simmered rather than boiled in the decade that was to follow.

Jordan returned to a political theme in *The Crying Game* a decade later, again using Rea in the starring role of a confused IRA man. It was a stylised mood-piece, pretentious in parts, but also oddly compulsive. And it had a whopper of a

suprise ending. It received six Oscar nominations.

The Crying Game made $60 million at the box office. Suddenly, the ex-Clontarf poet was on the map. The cheque books came out for *Interview With a Vampire*. He proved he could be trusted with a megabucks budget. The *Michael Collins* script was dusted down.

Liam Neeson was a veritable shoo-in for the eponymous role. At six foot four, he certainly had the height for The Big Fellow. He was also able to capture Collins' brash, feckless idealism. And he was a heart-throb of sorts. But a heart-throb with an earthy overlay.

'Sometimes I look at myself in the mirror,' he said self-deprecatingly, 'and I think I should be back home driving a forklift.' That too was important for getting into the heart of the part: the homespun edge. And the sense of mischievousness.

Liam Neeson in younger days.
(*Ballymena Guardian*)

Neeson's Oscar-nominated performance in *Schindler's List* effectively gave him the green light to play Collins. In many ways, the two heroes were similar: the German profiteer who grew rich on the spoils of war but also saved so many Polish Jews from the Nazi death camps possessed the same ambivalent allure as Collins, a man edged with a similarly blunt charisma. And, like Schindler, both villain and demi-god, depending on which side of the political spectrum you embodied. Ireland, after all, had had its own little holocaust.

Neeson had got to know Jordan as far back as John Boorman's *Excalibur* when the would-be director made a documentary on the shooting of that movie. It was exposure for Neeson, but blink and you missed him. Seven years later he was to team up with Jordan again, this time in the critically-maligned *High Spirits*, a confused mish-mash of necrophilia and slapstick. Neeson looked as uncomfortable here as any other member of the cast, but it gave the pair of them the opportunity to talk about the Collins project...again. There were many glitches to be ironed out, but Neeson assured Jordan he was there if he needed him.

In the years following, Neeson rarely forswore an opportunity to mention the project to any interviewer who cared to listen, hoping the resulting column inches would galvanise public reaction towards moving the project on another vital inch. Everybody knew it was in the offing, everybody wanted to see it get made; what was missing was somebody to come up with a lot of money. And a lot of faith. Jordan was a respected director with many earnest, if uneven, movies behind him, but the Collins project was always going to be a shot in the dark.

Michael Collins, after all, wasn't a Nixon or a Wyatt Earp. Maybe Oskar Schindler wasn't a household name before *Schindler's*

List, but Thomas Kennelly's novel about him was a best-seller. Could somebody write a best-seller about Michael Collins or had it all been said before? Eoghan Harris also had a script completed, and it looked like a race between himself and Jordan to see who would get their handiwork up on screen first.

Harris' script - originally read by Michael Cimino in 1985 - focused more on Collins the man rather than the astute political animal, and his relationship with Hazel Lavery ('a woman airbrushed out of his life by a long line of pious biographers' according to Harris) rather than Kitty Kiernan. A recent biography by Sinead McCoole claims Collins had a fiery affair with Lady Lavery in London in the weeks prior to his signing the Anglo-Irish Treaty. It also claims that her stabilising influence on Collins was directly related to his growing tendency to grasp the ballot box rather than the blunderbuss. 'Collins

Julia Roberts as Kitty Kiernan poses for photographers.
(*Copyright: The Star*)

without Hazel was like Hamlet without Ophelia,' Harris contended. Kitty Kiernan, in contrast, had more of a girl-next-door appeal for him.

Nonetheless, Harris' script proved too hot to handle at the end of the day and Jordan's more standard work held sway with the money men.

For the sometime prize-winning novelist and quixotic director, it was time to re-investigate a personal obsession.

A young Liam Neeson relaxes off the set.
(*Ballymena Guardian*)

ACTION!

'The game's over, Harry - we've lost again'

It's 1916 in the G.P.O. and it looks like the old, old story as a distraught Collins addresses his friend Harry Boland. The rising has just been quashed. Another Paradise Postponed for the insurrectionists, by all accounts...

Our history books stopped at this juncture, making the Civil War that ensued into little more than a footnote. Neil Jordan goes a step further, creating a hero who made his reputation in the aftermath of that watershed, bequeathing us a nation out of the ashes of the G.P.O.

It's a divided nation, however, a compromised settlement. De Valera has Collins do his dirty work for him in what effectively becomes a kamikaze trip to London. Collins observes presciently that he may have signed his death warrant at

Behind the scenes at City Hall.
(*Copyright*: A.*Flynn*)

the negotiating table. Such a prophecy comes to pass as the organisation he finetuned exacts a terrible revenge on him for his perceived capitulation. Neil Jordan captures such events in a montage that looks like a crash course in tribal memory.

The film explodes in your face like a Scud missile. Elegiac and blunt by turns, we have Collins swearing like at a stevedore's convention and then playing Sir Lancelot with his darling in a hotel bedroom. Men shake hands behind closed doors while outside in the streets a more naked fury erupts. A nation is born in the blood of uncertain martyrs while deals are struck and promises reneged upon. There's no logic in it, just the necessary horrors of a probably irresoluble conflict. The city of Dublin is recreated brick by brick and then razed to the ground as Jordan rewrites history on blazing celluloid.

He was working on his biggest budget thus

Past and present - getting ready to set up a scene.
(*Copyright: Jim Walpole Irish Sun*)

far, but by Hollywood standards it still wasn't excessive. A hitherto minimalistic operator, many wondered if he could handle crowd scenes, or epochal moments, with the same dexterity he had applied to stories about intense souls in lonely bedsits, or ponderous, unhistorical anti-heroes in brooding vignettes.

The answer was that he took to the big stage as one to the manner born. The great irony of the movie is that it proves Jordan is actually better off when prevented from indulging in (quasi?) existential soulsearching. Gothic motifs may work on the pages of experimental novels, but cinema is a different medium by far. Here, due to the massive historical overlay of the material at hand, Jordan has been unwilling - or unable - to indulge his twitchy penchants, and it proves to be the making of him. The great surge of public events curbs the wordy self-indulgence evident in much of his back catalogue.

Journalist Senan Molony and other extras.
(Copyright: The Star)

Filming a marching army on Dame St.
(Copyright: Neil Fraser, Irish Sun)

The texture of the film is rich. Jordan pulled an impish trick on his bank manager by recruiting thousands of extras free of charge in the middle of the shoot. People from all over the country thronged into Wicklow to be kitted out in period dress for scenes that would, in another film-maker's m.o., eat up the lion's share of his budget.

'If we had done it anywhere else,' he admitted, 'and under any other circumstances, it would have cost at least double the money. Virtually everyone worked to scale. All the money is up there on the screen.'

The cast looked impressive. Liam Neeson was just fresh from playing another national hero - Rob Roy. Substitute a military uniform for the kilt and you're halfway there. A kind of Don Corleone crossed with Finn McCool, he strode through the role like a Colossus.

Alan Rickman, an actor we all loved to

hate, was drafted in to play de Valera. Who else could capture a silver-tongued devil as smarmily as he?

Then there was Aidan Quinn, as solid a performer as Neeson any day of the week, but maybe not in the A-League yet. He would find it difficult to 'carry' a film, but you couldn't have anyone more reliable riding shotgun for you. Cue Harry Boland, Collin's best friend and the third element in the Collins/Kiernan love triangle.

There could only be one woman to play Kiernan. Julia Roberts was America's quintessential sweetheart before Sandra Bullock sneaked up on the blind side and divested her of that particular title, warming her way into the heart of John Q. Public. Kitty Kiernan looked like being the catalyst to put her back up there where she belonged. Some naysayers would claim she distracted (and detracted) from the plot, but Collins' involvement with her was too golden an opportunity to throw

up. Everybody in Ireland knew about it, even if only in an epistolary manner. Now that it was becoming visual, finally, we would see how Collins could bring another type of romance to Irish History.

Wooing her with a single red rose, Collins sweet-talks his darling in a hotel bedroom on the very same morning his men wipe out so many members of British Intelligence who are stalking him. 'Give us the future,' he demands, 'We have had enough of the past'. Upon such ostensibly casual comments did the dawn of a new era reside.

The era, however, accelerates his own date with destiny. He had always intuited that it would be his own who would turn on him, and so it came to pass. De Valera received an unlikely reprieve in 1916 and now Collins meets an equally unlikely nemesis.

The film was most noted for the aforementioned scene, heavily reminiscent of the end of *The Godfather*,

Soldiers relax off duty on the set.
(Copyright: The Examiner)

where Jordan intercuts love dialogue between Collins and Kiernan with the summary execution of various members of British Intelligence by Collins's allies. For some it was a cheap shot, for others a reverberative commentary on the manner in which the iconographic hero could be so deadly and yet so nonchalant. Perhaps it was this mixture that kept him alive so long when his name was on so many bullets.

One of those bullets eventually reached its target on a back road in Cork on August 22nd, 1922. Collins dies in the film as Kitty Kiernan shops for a wedding dress and Sinead O' Connor sings 'She Moves Through the Fair'. It's the end of an era in history, and also the end of a relationship that never really began.

For Jordan, the climax is almost Shakespearean. Collins is a man beset with a fatal contradiction. Like a reformed gunfighter who decides to take time out to

Garrett Flynn, an extra in the movie.
(*Copyright: Arthur Flynn*)

smell the roses, he realises it's already too late, that the die has long been cast.

He who lives by the sword shall die by it, but this swordsman had reformed; he had tried to re-invent himself, to embrace a new credo. A fiery Dionysius to De Valera's conniving Apollo, he becomes, in the end, a beautiful loser. The children of this world are wiser than the children of light, as De Valera - who has always had his eye fixed on the Main Chance - well knows.

The Long Fellow may outlast the Big Fellow, but the allure is gone. The good die young; the king is dead, long live the king.

The yob from West Cork has staked his place in the pantheon of Irish lore and it's left to De Valera - and Ireland - to pick up the pieces.

Relaxing after the shoot.
(Copyright: Neil Fraser, Irish Sun)

AFTERMATH

At the Venice Film Festival in August 1996, the film won the Golden Lion Award for Best Picture, with Liam Neeson scooping the Best Actor accolade. (Ironically enough, he wasn't able to collect it at the prescribed venue, having been rushed to hospital with an intestinal abscess. He was presented with it instead in a special bedside ceremony at the hospital). Jordan, as expected, won the coveted Leone d'Or Award to a standing ovation. There was so much overall excitement at the screening, one woman had a heart attack and died afterwards.

Not everybody was ecstatic, however. In *In Dublin*, Niall McDevitt wrote that the film was 'another example of the homogenised, pasteurised, sterilised cinema that Ireland is churning out like dairy produce these days'.

Liam Neeson chats to Michael D. Higgins.
(Copyright: The Examiner)

Others were even more vehement. Neeson's preponderance of expletives were blasted as being over-the-top and inaccurate, as was the 'massacre of the innocents' at Croke Park - and many commented that it was highly unlikely Collins would be engaged in nonchalant pillow talk with his sweetheart while his 'twelve apostles' were liquidating members of British Intelligence. Jordan's assertion that he took the gun out of Irish politics was also deemed myopic, as was his depiction of De Valera as a begrudging, mean-minded conniver. The visual spectacle of the movie, however, subdued such considerations, even if it didn't altogether remove them. When facts conflict the legend, as the man said, print the legend.

The British Press was especially hostile. One journalist asked Jordan if he felt the film would 'rattle the collection bins' for the IRA in the United States. Jordan felt the mere fact of asking such a question was to misunderstand the film. He had written, as he saw it, the story of a man who was part pugilist and part pacifist. Such a contradiction, he felt, reflected the Ireland of the time. In this sense, Collins was a microcosm of our national schizophrenia. Jordan denied his portrait of him was over-romanticised. 'Yesterday's terrorist is today's statesman', he said, cocking a snook at the revisionists.

He came in for a lot of stick from those who felt he had parlayed a disjointed historical perspective into the seminal events surrounding the founding of the state in a work that compromised truth to the commercial dictates of a celluloid blockbuster. The incensed director begged to disagree, informing all his detractors that he was an earnest historian - he had taken a degree in Irish History at UCD in the seventies - and had recreated the twenties as faithfully as he could, notwithstanding some negligible details. Imagining the film would help the cause of

The burned-out G.P.O.
(Copyright: *The Examiner*)

terrorists in America - or anywhere else - was to insult the public's intelligence.

Jordan was never in any doubt that his film would be inflammatory. He probably wouldn't have made it if it wasn't going to be. The challenge was in purveying a view of history that had an edge, an innovative spin. Did de Valera shaft Collins? Maybe the jury was still out on that one, but tongues would wag. And cash registers at the turnstiles would sing with the profits.

Eighty years on, the sons and grandsons of those who had been in the G.P.O. during the Easter Rising would play Civil War politics again in twee foyers of mutiplexes all round the country - if not the world. This was a story that wasn't going to go away; it had after all, birthed us a nation. For good and/or for ill. Yeats' terrible beauty was still gestating.

As well as being a tale of great historical moment, of course, *Michael Collins* is also a poignant love story. Collins' relationship with Kiernan, needless to say, had to feature, but some critics felt Jordan was again compromising his view of history by high-profiling the romantic subplot. Such a view misunderstood the nature of cinema as a medium, however. Every film, almost by definition, juggles with the facts. Whether it misrepresents them is another issue entirely.

Part of the problem with it, wrote Quentin Curtis, is that Jordan was trapped by the historical dimension of the script, and prevented from giving full vent to his huge creative gifts by the responsibility of the narrative. It worked best as a character study, he said. The film overall was a hybrid, 'often beautiful, sometimes evasive. Within its broad canvas, history, drama, biopic, *Boy's Own* adventure and romantic rivalry jostle for narrative precedence'.

Ciaran Carty of the *Sunday Tribune* put it well when he said that it was neither history nor a distortion of history: it was a film This may sound obvious, but it needed to be said.

More than anything else, what the film proved was that Michael Collins was still alive and well and living in the universal mind, a chameleon character whose life was as enigmatic as the events he shaped and which helped shape him. Nobody can verify the finer points of his relationship with De Valera, or Kitty Kiernan, or indeed Hazel Lavery, but the fact that he stands head and shoulders over his contemporaries both in his charisma and historical import was never in doubt, and it's this vibrancy the film celebrates.

Béal na mBláth may have caused the death of a man, but it begat a legend. Ní *fheichimid a leithéid arís.*